MOUNTAIN NAVIGATION

by

PETER CLIFF

Foreword by F. W. J. Harper, Principal of Glenmore Lodge,
National Mountaineering Centre.

First edition 1978.
Second edition 1980.

Silva Compasses reproduced by kind permission of Silva Compasses (U.K.).

Cover photograph: Tarmachen Ridge, Tayside, Scotland.

ISBN 0 9044 05 70 2

Printed in Great Britain by Diane E. Thompson,
16 Brandon Terrace, Edinburgh.

FOREWORD

Peter Cliff's book on Mountain Navigation is welcome because it brings together most of what can be taught about finding one's way around in the mountains.

I find it a very impressive piece of work due to the succinctness of his prose and the clarity of his explanation. He has avoided encumbering his text with inessentials, with the result that this seems to me to be the most useful book on Mountain or Hill Navigation available.

The book of course could not have been written without the benefit of the enormous experience of navigating and navigation instruction which Pete has with many different sorts of people. It is so worthwhile because of the lessons learnt from that experience.

I commend it to all those who wish to learn to find their way around mountains accurately and with confidence.

Fred Harper
Glenmore Lodge.

To my mother and father.

Introduction

Map Reading

The Compass

Estimating Time

Estimating Paces

The Altimeter

Bad Weather Navigation

Alpine Glacier Navigation

INTRODUCTION

The art of navigation has never been accorded the prominence it perhaps warrants in mountaineering.

While many notable mountaineers, particularly mountain explorers, have demonstrated brilliant feats of navigation, it has been only in other sports like ocean racing, ocean cruising, flying, hot air balooning, and orienteering that the navigator is recognised as an essential presence and is accorded status as such.

The recent development in Britain of schemes for training people to lead and instruct others in the hills has drawn attention to mountain navigation, because in those schemes considerable importance is attached to it. Many of the skills described in this book will be of particular value to people involved in those schemes.

Another important factor is Mountain Rescue statistics. A very high proportion of mountain accidents is due, directly or indirectly, to bad navigation. Accidents are often reported as being due to exposure, slipping on snow or grass, etc. etc.— but in many of these cases the accident would not have happened if the navigation had been good.

Mountain navigation is not done by map and compass alone. Look at shepherds, stalkers and ghillies—men who spend a lifetime in the hills and probably never use a map or compass. They use local knowledge and natural skills based on experience going back maybe generations. Possibly they have hidden skills similar to those of the ancient Polynesian navigators: skills which today are barely surviving. But for those of us without such ancestry, it seems we have two choices. Either we stay well within our limits by only going into easy hills and only in good weather conditions. Or we can develop skills in mountain navigation to such an extent that we can reasonably go into unfamiliar mountains in bad conditions.

This book describes those skills.

MAP READING

Mountain navigation can be thought of in two parts. The first part is map reading: i.e. the ability to look at the map and to be able to picture the ground in your mind. The second part is all the rest and includes use of the compass, estimating time, estimating paces, and use of the altimeter.

THE IMPORTANCE OF MAP READING

This first part, map reading, is the vital one. If you are good at this, you will only have to resort to the other skills in difficult conditions. Most of the time you can keep walking at a steady pace, having occasional quick looks at the map without breaking your step.

If you are on your own, there is nothing more pleasant than stopping whenever you want to look at the view or the map. But if you are the leader of a group, continual stops by you make life difficult for the rest of the group (particularly those at the back). They won't thank you for it, and they'll probably begin to wonder if you know where you are.

The ability to move at a steady pace while navigating over unfamiliar ground is the essence of mountain navigation; and, if you master this first part, map reading, you are most of the way there.

CONVENTIONAL SIGNS

The symbols used on maps are called conventional signs. It is unnecessary to learn them all parrot-fashion, as every map has them shown in the legend, which will be on the side or the bottom of the map.

As a mountaineer, I have not yet found it necessary to be able to distinguish between a church with a tower, one with a spire, or one with neither. On the other hand, if you are out in bad visibility and the map shows crags or cliffs in front of you, it is quite important to know whether, if you keep on walking, you will be at the top or the bottom of them. This conventional sign must be treated with caution as there are cases on the Ordnance Survey maps where it has been placed the wrong way round.

Again, it is a waste of time to learn all the roads and railways; and yet the ability to distinguish between a footpath and a parish boundary is quite useful. If you are colour blind on red and black, you won't be able to.

The most important conventional sign for the hillwalker and mountaineer is the contour line. This is a line on the map joining points of equal height. On the latest metric maps, the interval between them is 10 metres, they are coloured brown, and every fifth one is heavier (to make counting easier). Against each heavy contour there is, at some stage, a figure giving its height. To begin with, it is important to look at these heights in order to tell whether the slope is going up or down. With practice, your eye takes in the whole picture of the map and you can work it out without reference to the heights.

We will look at contour lines in more detail under 'Interpreting the Map'

GRID REFERENCES

British maps are covered with grid lines, lines running north/south and west/east on the map. Each line is numbered, and the squares formed by these lines are one kilometre squares (even on the 1″ maps). A system of four figure and six figure references is used to pinpoint positions.

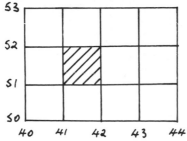

In Fig. (1) the shaded square is 4151. You go along the bottom first: it lies between 41 and 42. Then you go up the side: it lies between 51 and 52.

Fig. (1). Four figure grid reference.

2

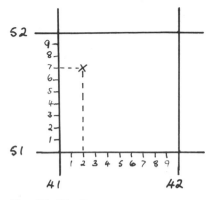

To get the six figure reference, the sides of the squares are split into tenths, using your compass or ruler. This gives the 3rd and 6th figure. In Fig. (2), point X is at 41**2** 51**7**.

Fig. (2). Six figure grid reference.

You always take the figures along the bottom first, and then go up the side. To help remember this: "You go in the door and along the hall before going up the stairs".

If you use a compass with a roamer (for example the Silva Type 4), working out a grid reference is very quick and easy.

1. Place the corner of the relevant roamer on the point, as shown in Fig. (3).

2. Read off the figures on the roamer, as indicated by the arrows in the diagram. In this case we get 41**4** 51**2**.

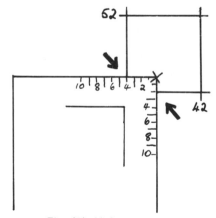

Fig. (3). Using a roamer for grid references.

Bear in mind that, just as a four figure reference covers a square (a one kilometre square), a six figure reference also covers a square. It is a smaller one, namely a 100 metre square. Your point could be anywhere within that 100 metre square.

SCALE

The scale of the map is the relationship between the distance on the map and the distance on the ground.

It might be expressed as, for example, "One inch to the Mile" which means that one inch on the map is equivalent to one mile on the ground. Since there are 63,360 inches to the mile, this scale could also be expressed as 1:63,360. This One Inch scale has now been replaced by the metric 1:50,000, which means that 1 centimetre on the map equals 50,000 centimetres on the ground (which is 500 metres).

Fig. (4). Photograph of Loganlea Reservoir.

In the photograph above, a house called 'The Howe' is shown in the bottom lefthand corner. If you were to walk from there along the far side of the reservoir, after 600 metres you would come to a stream and the final distance to the end of the reservoir is one kilometre.

4

Using a compass or ruler, measure the distance on the map (Fig. 5) between 'The Howe' and the end of the reservoir. You will find it is 2 centimetres.

On this map, therefore, 2 centimetres equal 1 kilometre on the ground. 1 centimetre is therefore 500 metres ground (which is 50,000 centimetres).

This map has a scale of 1:50,000.

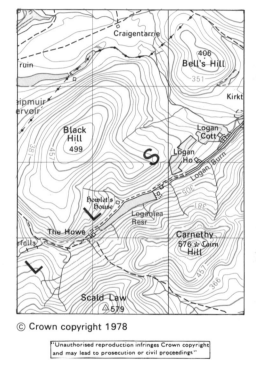

Fig. (5). Map of area in Fig. (4).

On the 1:50,000 scale one kilometre ground is shown by 2 centimetres on the map. If you want more detail, some areas are covered by the 1:25,000 where a kilometre on the ground is represented by four centimetres on the map—i.e. you get double the detail.

Fig. (6) and (7) show the same area on both scales.

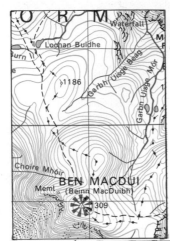

Fig. (6). 1:50,000

Note the extra detail on the 1:25,000, particularly the streams and lochans.

Fig. (7). 1:25,000

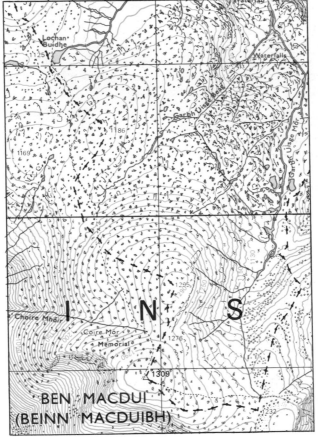

Changing from one scale to another can be difficult. Some areas in Britain were covered by both One Inch and Two-and-a-Half Inch. These have been superseded by the metric 1:50,000 and 1:25,000, although not all the popular mountain areas have yet been covered by the 1:25,000 series. If you are in an area which is covered by both series, it is quite possible to have both maps in your pocket, and the danger of forgetting which one you are using need not be exaggerated.

INTERPRETING THE MAP

The most important part of navigation is to be able to look at the map and to be able to picture the actual ground in your mind. The shape of the contour lines shows the shape of the hillside, and the spacing of them shows the steepness of the hillside. With practice, while looking at the map the photograph comes up in your mind. Once you can do this, you will be able to navigate accurately.

Fig. (8) shows a photograph of a hill and Fig. (9) shows the map of the same area. The photograph was taken from the top of Scald Law, looking north-east towards Carnethy Hill. If you look closely at the map you can identify the following features, and a comparison with the photograph shows the features in actual fact:

1. Going from Scald Law to Carnethy Hill there is a descent to a col or shoulder, followed by an ascent to Carnethy Hill.

2. For most of the descent from Scald Law the contour lines are evenly spaced, but at the end (just before the col) they are closer together. Where they are closer, the hill is steeper, which means that the col will be in an area of 'dead' ground and will therefore be invisible from the top of Scald Law.

3. On the ascent to Carnethy Hill, the contour lines are at first close together (steep ground); then they are much more spaced out (the easy angled flat ridge); and at the end they are closer together again (steeper).

4. Carnethy Hill has a flat easy angled South-West ridge. To the right of this the contour lines are close together, and they are bent through a right-angle. This shows a steeper slope with a recess like a stream.

5. The south ridge of Carnethy Hill has contour lines fairly close together all the way except for one section near the top where they are more spaced out. This shows a slope of uniform steepness except for the one section of less steep ground. On the photograph this is the slope which starts at the bottom righthand corner and goes straight to the top.

Fig (8). Photograph of Carnethy Hill.

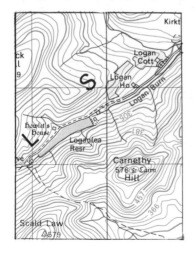

Fig. (9). Map of Carnethy Hill, scale 1:50,000.

© Crown copyright 1978

Figs. (10) to (15) show on the left-hand side the map of various typical mountain features, and on the right-hand side they are shown in elevation. You might find it good practice to cover the right-hand side and try drawing each in elevation on scrap paper.

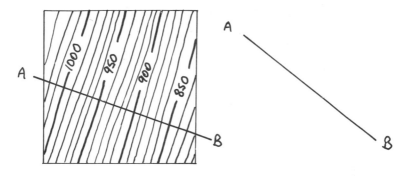

Fig. (10). An even slope

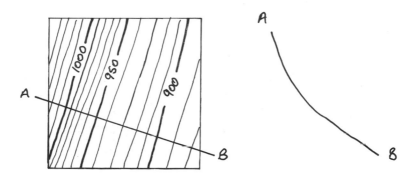

Fig. (11). A concave slope

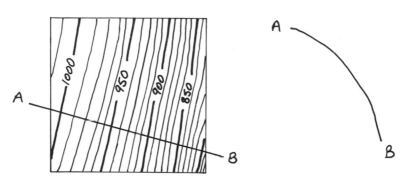

Fig. (12). A convex slope

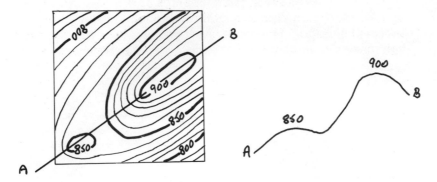

Fig. (13). A double top

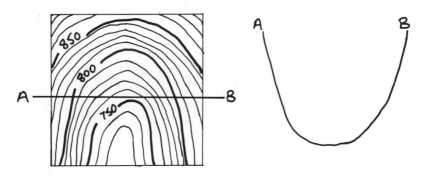

Fig. (14). A valley

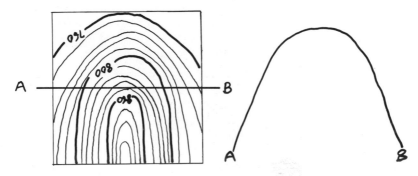

Fig. (15). A spur or ridge

The most obvious difference between Figs. (14) and (15) is that in Fig. (15) the figures indicating contour heights are upside down, whereas in Fig. (14) they are the right way up. This is intentional; and it gives an immediate indication of whether the slope goes up or down. If, when you look at the map, the figures are the correct way up, then low ground is towards the bottom of the map and high is towards the top. Conversely, if the figures are upside down, high ground is towards the bottom of the map and low is towards the top. In other words, to quickly tell whether the ground is going up or down, look to see which way up the writing is.

If you become good at interpreting the map and at picturing the actual ground in your mind, you will be able to:

1. expect what is coming, in terms of landcape. This in itself will help to keep you on course; and it will help you keep a steady pace with not too many stops to look at the map.

2. practice such basic concepts as:

i. keeping off ridges in high wind.

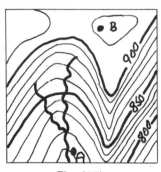

Fig. (16).

In fig. (16) there are two routes from A to B. One is up the ridge on the right; the other up the stream to the col, and then to B. In high winds the ridge would be dangerous, particularly in a gusting wind which is usual in Britain, and it would certainly be tiring. A more comfortable and safe route would be up the stream.

ii. keeping to ridges in heather and snow. When the valley floor is full of luxuriant heather, walking can be hard work. But the ridge will be swept bare by wind and conditions underfoot will always be easier. Snow is usually swept off ridges and it fills the lee slopes and the valley floors. Underfoot conditions in the valley could be snow to such a depth that you are sinking up to your waist, while on the ridge you'd be walking on exposed rocks with some hard snow and ice.

11

iii. avoiding dangerous slopes in avalanche conditions. The study of avalanches is a fascinating and complicated subject; and the standard book on the subjects "Snow and Avalanches" by Colin Fraser. The most common avalanche in this country is the windslab, which forms on lee slopes. If you are going to an area in winter, find out what the weather conditions (particularly wind) have been. If for example, there have been strong SW winds, avoid snow slopes facing NE.

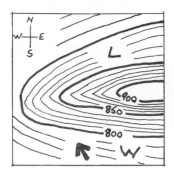

In Fig. (17) a SE wind would blow in the direction of the arrow. The northerly slope marked 'L' becomes a lee slope and is therefore suspect. The slope marked 'W' for windward is safer.

Fig. (17). Lee and windward slopes.

In Fig. (18), to descend from A to B in snow conditions, where windslab is suspect, there are four possibilities:

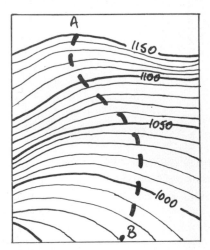

i. the slope on the left. Dangerous because it is convex, particularly at 1050m.—point of tension.

ii. direct line A to B. A uniform angle of slope, safer than the convex.

iii. the slope on the right. Concave, and usually the safest. But there could be windslab on the top steep bit.

iv. the dotted line is a compromise, taking the safest of each slope and avoiding the worst.

Fig. (18). Safest route on snow slope.

This small book is not the place to go into detail on snow and avalanches, but obviously successful winter navigation hinges on the ability to recognise different snow conditions.

THE COMPASS

TYPES OF COMPASS

There are two types of compass easily available to the hillwalker and mountaineer: the Prismatic and the Silva. The Prismatic is too heavy and complicated for our purposes. The Silva, on the other hand, is light, simple, and does everything necessary.

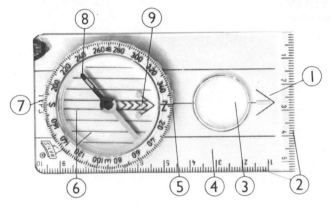

Fig. (19). Silva Compass Type 3.

1. Direction of travel arrow. 2. Scales. 3. Magnifying lense. 4. Transparent baseplate. 5. Read bearings here. 6. Orienting lines in compass housing. 7. Degrees dial, each calibration being 2°. 8. Red magnetic needle. 9. Orienting arrow.

Silva produce a wide range of compasses, and if you are going to buy one the following points may be useful:

—some have rulers in centimetres and millimetres only, as in fig. (19); some in inches also. In case you use a 1″ or 2½″ map, the latter is more useful.

—compass housing base plates may be solid or transparent. For lining up on grid lines on the map, the latter is easier.

—the degrees are either on the side or on the top of the compass housing. When on the top, they are easier to read.

—exchangeable scales are available, to slip over the front of the compass. These tend to get lost, and are not therefore recommended.

—the Ranger Type 15T, Fig. (20), enables bearings to be taken more accurately. This facility is, however, not really necessary for us, and the extra weight of this compass is therefore a disadvantage.

—a compass with a roamer is very useful. The one in Fig. (21) has a roamer for 1″, 1:50,000 and 1:25,000 maps. With this you can measure distances and work out grid references very quickly on any of these maps.

Fig. (20). Silva Ranger compass Type 15T

Fig. (21). Silva compass with roamer Type 4.

Fig. (22). Silva optical sighting compass, Type 54NL.

The Type 54NL is a more expensive compass, but it enables bearings to be taken accurately to ½ a degree. Again, it is lightweight; and is a really superb compass.

USES OF THE COMPASS

The Silva compass is a very versatile instrument and can be used for:

1. measuring distances on the map.
2. working out grid references.
3. finding north.
4. setting the map.
5. calculating bearings, map to compass, for following.
6. calculating bearings, compass to map, for:
   - i. identifying peaks etc.
   - ii. resections (cocked hats).
   - iii. aspects of a slope.

1. MEASURING DISTANCES ON THE MAP

If you have a compass with a roamer, as in Fig. (21) and (22), measuring distances, particularly those up to a kilometre, is very easy. If you don't have a roamer, you use the ruler on the compass, and this is where mistakes can happen.

The 1″ maps are easy enough.

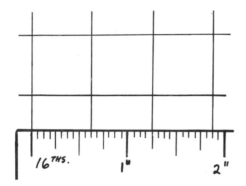

1″ equals 1 mile.
½″ equals 880 yards.
¼″ equals 440 yards.

one calibration on the ruler (i.e. one sixteenth) equals 110 yards. It also equals, for grid references, one tenth of a grid square.

Fig. (23). Measuring distances on 1″ map.

The metric maps can cause problems.

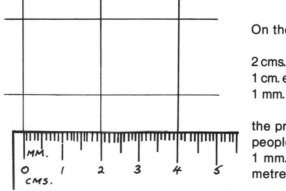

On the 1:50,000

2 cms. equal 1 kilometre.
1 cm. equals 500 metres.
1 mm. equals 50 metres.

the problem is that people often expect 1 mm. to equal 100 metres.

Fig. (24). Measuring distances on 1:50,000.

On the 1:25,000, 4 centimetres equal a kilometre, and one millimetre therefore equals 25 metres.

It is just a matter of familiarisation and practice; but it seems that this basic step causes a lot of errors and it cannot therefore be as easy as it appears.

2. WORKING OUT GRID REFERENCES

Again, if you have a roamer this is easy—see Fig. (3). If you don't have a roamer, it means using the ruler on the compass to split the kilometre square into tenths.

One Inch   use the inches ruler, as 10 calibrations (sixteenths) equal a kilometre and so there is one calibration for every tenth. See Fig. (23).

1:50,000   use the millimetre/centimetre ruler, as there are 2 calibrations (millimetres) for every tenth. See Fig. (24).

1:25,000   getting complicated, as on the millimetre/centimetre ruler it is 4 calibrations to a tenth, and on the inches ruler it is 2½. With either it is easy to count wrong.

3. FINDING NORTH

If you ask someone what the main use of a compass is, the answer will probably be: to find North. But in itself, this is not a great help, unless you are on the way by direct route to the North Pole. So, invariably this use of the compass is combined with one of the others.

There are in fact three norths in navigation—True, Grid and Magnetic.

True North: where the North Pole is and almost the same as Grid North. For hillwalking and mountaineering purposes, it can be ignored.

Grid North: the north to which the grid lines of the map point.

Magnetic North: because of the Earth's magnetism, the needle of the compass gets pulled over to one side. In Britain it is pulled about 7°-8° to the West, and in the Alps about 3° to the West. It is called Magnetic Variation.

Magnetic variation varies from place to place, and from year to year. On the map, among the conventional signs, the difference between Grid and Magnetic north will be shown.

For example: "Magnetic North: about 8½°W. of Grid North, in 1971, decreasing by about ½° in eight years." For 1979 the difference on that particular map will be 8°.

If you lose your compass, you can find north by other methods. They are not very accurate, but for interest's sake here are the two most well known ones, (a) by watch and sun, (b) by the stars.

By watch and sun:

—hold the watch flat in your hand.
—point the hour hand at the sun (ignore the minute hand).
—bisect the angle between 12 o'clock and the hour hand. This points south.

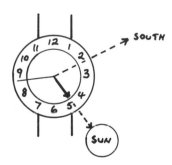

Fig. (25). Finding north by watch and sun.

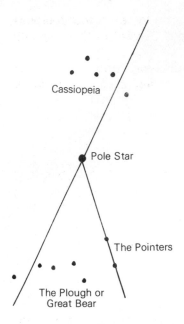

By the stars:

—the Plough revolves round the Pole Star; but wherever it is, its pointers point to the Pole Star.

—Cassiopeia is the same distance on the other side of the Pole Star, shaped like a flat W or M.

Fig. (26). Finding north by the stars.

4. SETTING THE MAP

This means getting the top of the map pointing north, so that the features on the map coincide with those on the ground. If you are facing south, it will mean that the writing on the map is upside-down.

There are two ways of doing this:

(a) **By Landmarks.** If you know where you are and can recognise landmarks, line up landmarks on the map with those on the ground. This will result in the top of the map pointing north.

(b) **By Compass** —hold the compass flat, so that the magnetic needle points steadily north.

—line up the map underneath the compass, with the grid lines parallel to the magnetic needle.
—the map is now pointing north.
—for practical purposes magnetic variation can be ignored.

When the map is correctly set, identify on the map the position you are at. If it shows on the map that there are, for example, crags high up on the slope on the right, then a look at the slope on the right will prove they are there. Setting the map means that you can pick out from the map any features, and by looking in that direction you can then identify them on the ground.

5. BEARINGS, MAP TO COMPASS

This is the more usual use of the compass. If you want to travel in bad visibility, take the bearing from the map, put it onto the compass, and then follow the compass. In the first part, measuring the bearing on the map, the compass is being used as a protractor.

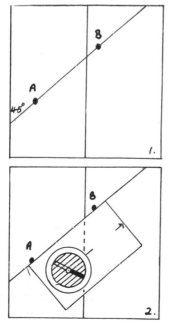

The steps are:
1. hold the map flat (it doesn't matter which way it is pointing). Estimate the bearing by eye. This avoids getting it 180° wrong. In the example it is about 45° when going from A to B.

2. place one long edge of the compass along the imaginary line AB with the direction of travel arrow pointing the way you want to go.

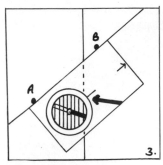

3. turn the compass housing until the orienting lines in the compass housing are parallel to the grid lines on the map. Read off the bearing at the point marked by the arrow. This is a grid bearing.

Fig. (27). Measuring a bearing on the map.

4. Because the magnetic needle is pulled off to one side, we must allow for this by adding the relevant magnetic variation. To remember whether to add or to subtract the variation, here are three aids:

   i   "add for Mag., get rid for Grid".

   ii   "Grid unto Magnetic, Add—GUMA".

        "Magnetic unto Grid, Subtract—MUGS".

   iii The landscape is bigger than the map, therefore the bearing for the landscape (magnetic) should be bigger than that for the map (grid).

In this case, we have a Grid bearing and we therefore add the magnetic variation ("Add for Mag") to make it magnetic. If the Grid bearing for example is 50° and the magnetic variation is 8°, the Magnetic bearing is 58°. Turn the compass housing until you have this on the compass.

5. In order to follow the compass, hold it flat in your hand in front of you. Now turn round until the red end of the magnetic needle points to North on the compass housing and is parallel to the orienting lines.
It is now correctly aligned.
The direction in which to go is shown by the Direction of Travel Arrow.

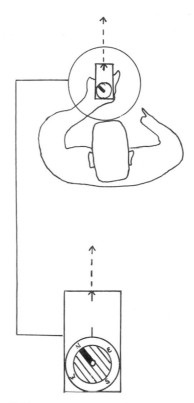

Fig. (28). Aligning the compass.

When aligning the compass, be very careful that there is no metal near you as it will affect the needle of the compass. Such things as ice axes, watches, tins of food, karabiners, etc. may affect it. Standing on an iron bridge has disastrous results; and occasional haywire navigation by military personnel has been attributed to keen soldiers holding the compass to their eyes, without realising that the metal plate behind their cap badge is playing havoc with the magnetic needle.

ERRORS WHEN TAKING BEARINGS, MAP TO COMPASS

When taking the bearing from the map, it is quite easy to be one calibration wrong, which gives an error of 2°. If you then try to follow that bearing in conditions of high wind and rain or snow, you may be another 4° out. The cumulative error is now 6°.

The effect of a 6° error is that, over a leg of 500 metres you are 52 metres out; over a leg of one kilometre you are 105 metres out; and over a leg of one and a half kilometres you are 157 metres out. The percentage, on a 6° error, is just over 10% (Fig. 29).

In conditions of stress an inexperienced navigator will be very lucky to be within 6°.

Even for an experienced navigator, this error has serious consequences. If the visibility is only 20 metres and you miss the point by over 100 metres, there is not much chance of seeing it. If, on the other hand, you know when you should be there, you can stop and start a sweep search—hence the importance of estimating time and paces. This is dealt with in more detail in the chapter 'Bad Weather Navigation'.

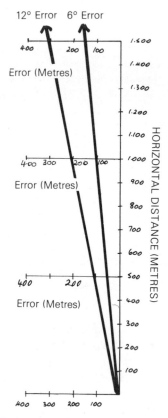

Fig.(29). Effect of 6° and 12° errors on a compass bearing.

6. BEARINGS, COMPASS TO MAP

There are three occasions when you might want to take a bearing with your compass and convert it to the map.

1. **In order to identify a peak etc.** You might be able to identify it by setting the map and seeing what's there; but if this is not accurate enough, use the compass as follows:

i. holding the compass flat, point the direction of travel arrow at the peak.
ii. turn the compass housing until the orienting arrow in the housing lies underneath the magnetic needle and the red end of the magnetic needle points to North on the housing.
iii. read off the bearing.
iv. subtract magnetic variation to get a grid bearing ("Get rid for grid").
v. lay the compass on the map (it doesn't matter which way the map is pointing because you are now using the compass as a protractor), with one of the long sides on the point you are at (Point A in Fig. 30) and with the orienting lines in the compass housing parallel to the grid lines on the map, and the orienting arrow to North.

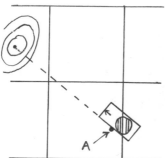

Somewhere along the side of the compass, and the continuation of that line, is the peak (dotted line in Fig. 30).

Fig. (30). Identifying an object.

2. **Resections ("Cocked Hats").** While the use of resections or back bearings to make "Cocked Hats" is useful in, for example, coastal navigation, it is a vastly overrated skill in mountain navigation. This is because, if you are lost, it is unlikely that you will be able to positively identify the two or three points necessary to do one. On the other hand, the taking of just one back bearing is something which is done fairly often.

The steps in making a resection are:

i. select at least two, and preferably three, points which you can positively identify and which are at widely different angles from you.

ii. with the first point go through steps 1-4 of 'In order to identify a peak'—i.e. take its bearing and convert to grid.

iii. put one long side of the compass on the point (point X in Fig. 31) with the orienting lines parallel to the grid lines and the orienting arrow pointing north on the map.

iv. you are somewhere along the side of the compass and the extension of that line.

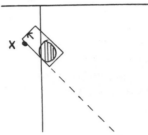

Fig. (31). Resection

v. repeat with the other two points (points Z and Y in Fig. 32). A 'Cocked Hat' is formed, with your position in the middle (point A).

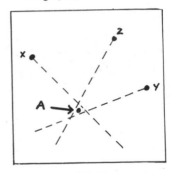

Fig. (32). A full resection.

There is a second method of using backbearings. Take the bearing of the first point and convert to grid (say 280° in Fig. 33).

Subtract 180° to get a backbearing of 100°. If you cannot subtract the 180°, then add it. For instance, the backbearing of 20° is 200°. Now lay the compass on the map as in Fig. (33) with a bearing of 100°, with the orienting lines parallel to the grid lines, and with the orienting arrow pointing to north on the map. You will be somewhere along the side of the compass

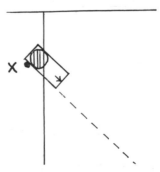

Fig. (33). Backbearing

and the extension of that line. Repeat with the other two points for a 'Cocked Hat'.

This could be said to be a purer and safer method, as the bearing is from the known point, and the direction of travel arrow is pointing to where you are. In practice, however, the first method is obviously quicker as there are less stages involved. Since there are less stages, there is less chance of making a mistake.

A full resection using three points is seldom done in mountain navigation. If you can identify three points, the weather must be clear, and in clear weather we seldom need such precision. Using one point, however, is done fairly often. The situation can arise where your approximate position is already defined by an obvious physical feature (e.g. you are following a ridge, a stream, a glacier, the edge of a forest etc.).

Presume you are on the crest of a ridge, as in Fig. 34, but you are not sure how far along it you are. The cloud suddenly lifts for a few seconds and you see a stream junction on your left. Take a bearing on it, and you can put your position at A.

Fig. (34). Fixing position by backbearing and feature.

3. **Aspect of the slope.** Imagine you have been out for some time in really bad visibility, that your last known point was half-an-hour away, and that the slope you are traversing is getting too steep for comfort. A very useful thing to do in this situation is to take the aspect of the slope.

The steps are:

i. point the compass down the slope and take the bearing. Convert to grid.
ii. put the compass on the map. Keeping the orienting lines in the compass housing parallel with the grid lines on the map, and

keeping the orienting arrow pointing north on the map, slide the compass along your presumed route.

iii. watch the long side of the compass carefully, because when it crosses the contour lines at right angles it means that the compass is pointing down the slope. You are on this slope.

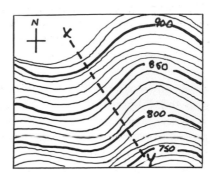

In Fig. (35), the slope XY has an aspect of 150° grid.

Fig. (35). Aspect of the slope.

Usually it is possible to confirm your position by continuing on the traverse. The map will show that the slope changes to a different aspect. When this happens, you have fairly accurate confirmation of your position.

This 'aspect of the slope' can also be used in a different situation. Presume that in Fig. (36) you want to get onto the slope marked A, that the slope marked X is for one reason or another dangerous (e.g. windslab), and that you are approaching from the south. If the visibility was very bad, it would be quite easy to stray on to slope X. But if you take the aspect of slope A from the map, and then work your way onto it by continually pointing your compass down the slope, you will be quite safe. In the example, slope A has an aspect of approximately 150°, whereas slope X is approximately 225°.

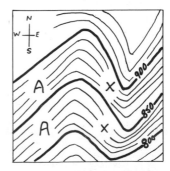

Fig. (36). Aspect of the slope.

28

ESTIMATING TIME

If you want to be a good mountain navigator, you must be able to judge how long it will take to get from one point to another, with various types of terrain, various weather conditions and various companions.

It can be thought of in two degrees of accuracy: general and detailed. By general I mean the ability to plan a route for the time available, given the particular conditions of weather and underfoot. You think in terms of half-hours, and probably keep an open mind as to the exact route until you actually get up there. By detailed I mean the ability to estimate a section within minutes; and to be accurate within 3-4 minutes over a half-hour section.

Few would disagree with the good sense of the first one, the general accuracy. As to the second one, the detailed accuracy, this has the following advantages:

—it helps your general accuracy.
—if you arrived in the dark at the top of a climb, it might be useful to help find the top of the easy descent route.
—in total darkness or white-out it gives you an essential dimension. It tells you how far you have gone, and when combined with accurate compass work it means you can navigate in these conditions. You may choose not to go out in these conditions, but there is always the chance of being caught out in them.

NAISMITH'S RULE

This is the classic rule for estimating time. It is: 3 m.p.h. + ½ hour for every 1000 ft. climbed. In metric terms, this is 5 k.p.h. + ½ hour per 300 metres.

As a general guide it is a useful and easily remembered rule. Be careful to take into account every ascent and descent. For example, you ascend 100 metres, descend 50 metres, and finally ascend 70 metres. The overall difference is an ascent of 120 metres; but the estimate must be worked out on 170 metres, since this is the amount actually climbed.

When counting contour lines, every fifth one is a heavier line. Count these, and then the individual ones at either end. This is much quicker than counting each individual line. Some people work out the height they are at, the height they are going to, and find the difference. Again, this is invariably slower than counting the heavy contour lines plus the individual ones at either end.

Obviously, though, the time taken will vary according to a number of variables. For instance:

—fitness of the party (for example, inexperienced children as compared to experienced adults).
—loads carried (day sacs or 50 lb. ones with tents).
—conditions underfoot (deep heather as against a ridge or path; deep snow as against hard snow).
—weather conditions (a strong wind behind or against you).

These variables are not taken into account by Naismith's Rule.

Tranter's Variation to Naismith's Rule

Tranter's Variation takes into account these variables, and is an interesting study. Before using the chart (Fig. 37) you have to first of all establish your fitness level. In the case of a group, you take the fitness level of the slowest.

The fitness level is: the time taken to climb 1000 ft. (300 metres) in ½ mile (800 metres) when fresh, at a normal pace and with no rests. Suppose this takes you 30 minutes, then your fitness level is 30.

Fitness Level	Time taken in hours according to Naismith's Rule															
	2	3	4	5	6	7	8	9	10	12	14	16	18	20	22	24
15	1	1½	2	2¾	3½	4½	5½	6¾	7¾	10	12½	14½	17	19½	22	24
20	1¼	2¼	3¼	4½	5½	6½	7¾	8¾	10	12½	15	17½	20	23		
25	1½	3	4¼	5½	7	8½	10	11½	13¾	15	17½					
30	2	3½	5	6¾	8½	10½	12½	14½	TOO MUCH TO							
40	2¾	4¼	5¾	7½	9½	11½		BE ATTEMPTED								
50	3¼	4¾	6½	8½												

Fig. (37). Tranter's Variations.

Example: you plan a trip of 10 kilometres, with a vertical height gain of 600 metres. By Naismith's Rule the estimate for this would be 3 hours. If your fitness level is 30, Tranter's estimate is 3½ hours.

Tranter's chart not only takes into account the fitness of the party. It also caters for the other variables:

—loads carried: drop one fitness line for every 30 lbs.
—conditions underfoot: drop one or two fitness lines for the ground, and up to four for snow.
—weather: drop one fitness line for night, bad visibility or strong winds.

FLATTISH, UNDULATING GROUND

In practice, few people know their 'fitness level' for Tranter's chart, so the navigator ends up guessing it. There are other ways of estimating time, and the ones you use are a matter of choice. Some, however, are more suitable for particular types of terrain. The most difficult terrain for navigation is flattish, undulating terrain with few features. If you are climbing or descending steeply, there is probably a clearly defined feature to help you (like a well-defined ridge or stream). But on flat, undulating ground it is very useful to be able to estimate time accurately; and the following methods are suggested.

1. **Naismith's Rule.** This can be used for the first leg, and the subsequent estimates adjusted as you see how fast you are going.

2. **Horizontal Distance Only.** In this kind of terrain it is possible to ignore the small amounts of ascent and descent, and to work out an estimate using the horizontal distance only.

Formulas:
—1,000 yds. (900 metres) + small uphill = 20 mins.
—1,000 yds. (900 metres) + small downhill = 15 mins.

Having seen on the first section how fast you are going, subsequent estimates can be based on these formulas, together with necessary adjustments.

3. **Timing Charts.** After the first leg, you will have an idea as to the speed you are going, perhaps 2 m.p.h. or 3 k.p.h., and from then on you can use that column on the charts below.

Yards	M.P.H.				Metres	K.P.H.			
	3	2½	2	1		5	4	3	2
1760	20	25	30	60	1000	12	15	20	30
1000	12¼	16	20	40	800	10	12	16	24
880	10	12½	15	30	700	9	11	14	21
500	6	8	10	20	500	6	7½	10	15
440	5	6¼	7½	15	400	5	6	8	12
220	2½	3¼	4	7½	200	2½	3	4	6
100	1¼	1¾	2	4	100	1¼	1½	2	3

Fig. (38). Timing Charts.

Example: the first leg is 400 metres and it takes 8 minutes. If the next leg is 700 metres, use the 3 k.p.h. column and estimate 14 minutes.

Always be prepared to revise your estimate. For example, if you find the snow has changed from breakable crust to hard wind-blown snow, you will move much faster. If someone stops to fasten a cagoule, don't forget to add that time to the estimate.

The Timing Charts can be carried in a small plastic wallet on a string round the neck. When under pressure (for example, high wind, rain or snow, bad visibility, and a group relying on you to navigate) all you have to do is to measure the distance on the map and then read off a figure from the chart. It is quick and easy; and it avoids having to work things out in these difficult conditions when a mistake is easily made.

ASCENT OF STEEP GROUND

As already mentioned, there will probably be some clearly defined physical feature to help navigation (e.g. a well-defined ridge or stream), and so accurate timing is not so necessary. Three useful methods are:

1. **Naismith's Rule.** A fit group may climb at two-thirds of Naismith's Rule, and with practice you can become fast at working it out.

Example: horizontal distance of 2 kilometres plus a climb of 450 metres.
    2 kilometres at 5 k.p.h. = 24 minutes.
    450 metres at ½ hour per 300 metres = 45 minutes.
    Total for Naismith = 69 minutes (two-thirds = 46 minutes).

It is useful to break Naismith's Rule down as follows:

Horizontal:	5 kilometres	= 60 mins.
	1 kilometre	= 12 mins.
Vertical:	300 metres	= 30 mins.
	100 metres	= 10 mins.
	50 metres	= 5 mins.

As you can see from the above breakdown, Naismith's Rule allows an extra 5 minutes for every 50 metres climbed. On the map every fifth contour line (i.e. every 50 metres) is a heavier line. Allow, therefore, 5 minutes for every heavy contour line you cross.

Example: horizontal distance of 3½ kilometres plus a climb of 500 metres.

    3½ kilometres at 5 k.p.h. = 42 mins.

    500 metres is 10 heavy contour lines, which = 50 mins.

    Total = 92 mins.

2. **Vertical Height Only**: time allowance for height interval. On a steady climb (no hands and knees required, but a steady climb with some zig-zagging), you can ignore the horizontal distance and work off the vertical height gain.

A fit party with good conditions will climb 1,500 feet (500 metres) in an hour. This can easily be reduced to 1,000 feet (300 metres) in an hour, and this is more like the average. Time the first leg, and thereafter it is very quick and easy using this method.

This can be combined with the technique of counting heavy contour lines. 500 metres an hour becomes 10 heavy contour lines an hour; and 300 metres an hour becomes 6 heavy contour lines an hour.

3. **Vertical Height Only**: time allowance for each contour line. A time of 1½ to 3 minutes should be allowed for each contour line to be crossed. This amounts to the same as 2. above, and it is just a different way of doing it.

Methods 2. and 3. are quick and easy; and with practice are very accurate. Since less calculations are required than with Naismith's Rule, they are to be recommended.

DESCENT OF STEEP GROUND

There will probably be a clearly defined feature to help the navigation; and in practice it never seems to be so important to estimate time when going downhill.

The following formula is a useful one:

—3 m.p.h. + 10 mins. per 1,000 ft. descended.

—5 k.p.h. + 10 mins. per 300 metres descended.

PRACTICE

Without practice your estimates of time will be more of a hindrance than a help. It can be quite fun practicing, partularly on those days when you cannot see anything anyway.

Keep the sections, or legs, short by using natural features. Those taking 20-45 minutes are best.

A group of 10-12 people together can have a very useful time with a different person setting the pace for each leg. The others will be able to experience the problems of checking someone else's navigation. The need to change the estimate after the first few minutes will be obvious, as the new leader's pace is seen.

At the beginning of the day, estimates will vary and will be inaccurate. But after 8-10 sections, most estimates will be accurate within 3-4 minutes over a 30 minute leg.

ESTIMATING PACES

If you are navigating in very difficult conditions, for example a very dark night or a bad white-out, it is essential to move from one known point to another keeping the legs short—preferably not more than 400 yards, and certainly not more than a kilometre. In this situation, the ability to estimate how many paces you will take can be a useful aid. Combined with an estimate of time, you will know how far along the compass course you have gone.

Ascending or descending steep ground, it is not worth doing, as the inevitable zig-zags make it innacurate. But over flattish, undulating ground it can be very accurate, with practice. Some people, particularly orienteers, develop this skill to a very high degree, to the extent that they can estimate paces for any kind of ground and they rely on this rather than on estimating time.

The first thing to do is to try yourself out over a measured distance, say 100 metres. An average figure for a man over flat good going is 120 paces for 100 yards (90 metres). Many people prefer to think of these as double paces, so 120 paces is 60 double paces. This obviously means that half the amount of counting is necessary, consequently making the arithmetic easier.

Provided the ground is flattish and undulating, you can take the horizontal distance and multiply this by 3/2.

Example: 1,000 yds. x 3/2 = 1,500 paces.
900 metres x 3/2 = 1,350 paces.

You might find that multiplying by 6/5 or 5/3 is more accurate. It depends on the length of your stride and on the conditions. If you have a normal stride, a quick method of estimating double paces is to take the horizontal distance in metres, multiply by 6 and divide by 10.

Inevitably, round the 600 or 700 mark, someone asks you a question and you lose count. Silva produce a counter called a Tachometer, like the one illustrated in Fig. 39.

It goes up to 10, and can be used for counting the hundreds. It fixes easily on the side of the compass by drilling a small hole and gluing.

Fig. (39). A Tachometer.

Alternatively, a handful of small pebbles can be used.

Practice. Unless you practice, you will not have the confidence to use this technique. On the other hand, if you do practice it, it means that when the situation arises you have another technique to help your navigation.

No-one is suggesting we should all go round counting paces the whole time. The occasions when this technique might be used are very infrequent ones; but by definition they are very difficult and serious ones.

EXERCISES ON ESTIMATING TIME AND PACES

Using any of the suggested formulas, work out estimated times and paces for the following examples. Presume a small group of fit adults with light rucsacks. For numbers 15-19, do not bother with an estimate for paces as they are either ascents or descents of steep ground. Metric equivalents are in the next chart.

Example: In the first one, using Naismith's Rule, estimated time is 32 minutes. Reduce that a little for the fitness of the group; and it actually took 29 minutes. For estimating paces, if you take 6/5 x yards you get an estimate of 1848. It actually took 1900 paces. So the estimate in both cases is very accurate. The answers are on page 49.

No.	Distance (yards)	Height ± (feet)	Terrain	Visibility	Estimated Time	Paces
1	1540	+465	Good	Good	32	1900
2	1300	−150+250	Good	Good		
3	1760	−1088	Boulders	Good		
4	1760	+250	Good	Bad		
5	1320	−500	Boulders	Good		
6	770	+150	Heather	Good		
7	1320	−250	Good	Bad		
8	1000	−250	Good	Good		
9	1000	+150	Good	Good		
10	1860	+100	8″ snow	Good		
11	1000	+250	8″ snow	Mod.		
12	1320	Nil	snow & rocks	Good		
13	Returning in steps made in No. 12					
14	880	+100	Good	Good		
15	1320	+700	snow & rocks	Good		
16	650	+530	Good	Good		
17	1200	+1100	Good	Good		
18	880	−450	Icy	Good		
19	650	−530	Good	Good		

METRIC EQUIVALENT

No.	Distance (metres)	Height ± (metres)	Terrain	Visibility	Estimated Time	Paces
1	1405	+140	Good	Good	32	1900
2	1185	−45+75	Good	Good		
3	1610	−330	Boulders	Good		
4	1610	+75	Good	Bad		
5	1205	−150	Boulders	Good		
6	700	+45	Heather	Good		
7	1205	−75	Good	Bad		
8	900	−75	Good	Good		
9	900	+45	Good	Good		
10	1700	+30	8″ snow	Good		
11	900	+75	8″ snow	Mod.		
12	1205	Nil	snow & rocks	Good		
13	Returning in steps made in No. 12					
14	805	+30	Good	Good		
15	1205	+215	Good	Good		
16	590	+140	Good	Good		
17	1005	+335	Good	Good		
18	805	150	Icy	Good		
19	590	−140	Good	Good		

THE ALTIMETER

Altimeters are particularly useful in the following situations:

—Traversing. If traversing round a hill in bad visibility, most people have a tendency to lose height. If you are aware of this, you may over-correct the other way. An altimeter keeps you right.

—Featureless Terrain. A very typical Scottish terrain is the gently rising hillside which is littered with hillocks and peatbogs. On a bad day it can take a couple of hours to get across 4-5 kilometres of this stuff, and although you keep a good compass bearing, it is difficult to know how far across you are. A compass bearing plus altimeter tells you exactly. The estimates on time and pacing will be thrown by the hillocks and peatbogs. (Fig. 40).

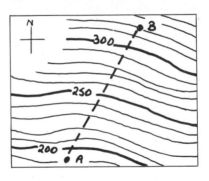

Example:
Set off from point A, which is a known point, on a bearing of 30°. When the altimeter reads 320 metres, you will be at point B.

Fig. (40). Use of altimeter in featureless terrain.

—Ridges. If you are going up or down a well-defined ridge, a compass bearing is unnecessary if you keep to the crest of the ridge. But it can be difficult to tell in bad visibility how far along the ridge you have gone. An accurate estimate of time will help, but an altimeter is simpler and more accurate. (Fig. 41).

Example:
If you keep to the crest of the ridge, when the altimeter reads 780 metres you will be at point A.

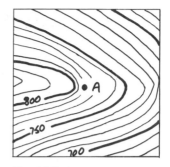

Fig. (41). Use of altimeter on a ridge.

—Glaciers. An altimeter is invaluable on glaciers, especially when descending fast on skis. See the next chapter 'Alpine Glacier Navigation'.

There are several types of altimeter on the market.

Fig. (42) shows one of the cheaper ones. Since each calibration is 200 feet, it is a useless instrument for accurate mountain navigation. It can be used as a barometer.

Fig. (42). An altimeter.

The Swiss made Thommen altimeter Fig. (43) is the best, but it is also rather expensive. It is small, easy to read, very reliable and strongly made. Each calibration is ten metres and it is possible to be accurate to this degree. Full instructions come with the instrument, but the following points are worth noting.

Fig. (43). Thommen Altimeter.

41

Points to note in using an altimeter

1. Since it works off barometric pressure the altimeter is affected by changes in the weather. It must be continually adjusted by resetting it at known points. If you know, for example, that a trough of low pressure is coming through, be careful about this point.

2. For the same reason, if you go for more than 10 kilometres horizontal distance or for more than 500 metres vertical height without resetting it, it may be inaccurate.

3. The speed at which you travel is important. If you are moving slowly, it could take you 2 hours to cover 5 kilometres horizontal distance; and two hours is more than enough for pressure to change and for the instrument to be inaccurate.

4. The altimeter is affected by temperature changes. There is a complicated procedure for correcting this, but provided you reset regularly on known points, this can be (and in practice invariably is) ignored.

5. Method of use. If, for example, you are going from A (height 500 metres) to B (height 800 metres), make sure that at A the altimeter is reading 500 metres. If it is not, adjust the setting so that it does. When you get to B, it will read 800 metres. When at B, a small adjustment due to barometric pressure or temperature may be necessary. Be sure to make this adjustment before continuing, because otherwise they become cumulative.

6. In the hut or tent, you can use it overnight as a barometer. Either set it to zero or to the height of the hut. If in the morning, the instrument shows the height of the hut to be higher than it actually is, the pressure has dropped. If it shows the height to be lower, the pressure has risen.

BAD WEATHER NAVIGATION

When the weather is fine, particularly when the visibility is clear, navigation can be done quickly and effectively by map-reading alone. But in conditions of bad weather, the other skills (compass, estimating time and paces, and altimeter) are very necessary, and at any one time you probably use a selection of those techniques. In addition to what has already been said about these skills, there are one or two other factors which can help navigation in very bad conditions.

1. Preparation. Time spent in the hut or in the tent looking at the map and the intended route is time very well spent.

2. Route Card. Have you ever tried taking a bearing off a map in a Force 8 wind? It is difficult, and the chance of error is great. It is much better to do it in the comfort of the hut or tent and to memorise it in the form of a short route card. Avoid long-winded route cards. Keep them short with the minimum of essential information.

Example: you will be coming to a col which obviously will be exposed to a high wind and blizzard. The hut is not far from the col. The place to work out the bearing is down below the col—not up in the blizzard.

'East end of col to hut 68°M. 650m. + 70m. est. 20 mins.'

With that information written down on a piece of paper, you will be able to move straight off the col and onto the hut without stopping.

3. Make sure you have easy access to everything.
—buy a map which is sealed on both sides for waterproofing. Alternatively, cover it with transposeal, or keep it in a polybag.
—if you continually use one area, cut the map up for just that area. It will then be small and easy to use.
—keep the compass on a wrist or neck loop. The neck loop seems preferable, as it leaves the hands free; but it must be long enough so that it can be used with the map.

—keep any timing charts and formulas for estimating time and paces in a small plastic wallet round your neck, or fix to the back of the map.

—have an anorak with a map pocket.

4. Appoint a back-marker, preferably someone responsible and in easily recognisable clothing, to keep the group together.

5. Navigation checker. In conditions of white-out or other bad visibility, put someone in third position to check your navigation. If they are right behind you in second position, it is difficult for them to check that you are following a compass bearing correctly. On the other hand, if they are too far back, you will be out of touch and it results in shouting and misunderstanding.

6. Man-out-in-front. If you find it difficult to follow a compass bearing, put someone out in front of you and use him as a reference point. This has the same purpose as asking someone in third position to check your bearing, but the man-out-in-front method is usually more chaotic as you have to continually tell him where to go.

7. Aiming-off.

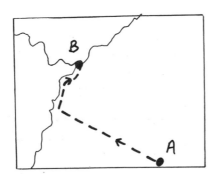

Fig. (44). Aiming-Off.

In the example you are going from A to the stream junction at B. If you take a direct bearing, you might miss it (ref. Fig. 44), and not know on which side you missed it. By deliberately aiming-off to below the junction, and then following the stream up to it (the dotted line), you are sure of success.

8. Attack points. Orienteers use attack points as a matter of course, and this technique can be used effectively in mountain navigation. Identify on the map the point to which you are heading. If this is an indistinct point, pick out a more distinct point

44

nearby, one which will be clearly identifiable once you get there and one which is easy enough to reach. This is the attack point. Navigate to the attack point, and then go on to your point. If you fail to find your point, return to the attack point and try again.

9. Rope-up. If there is a risk of falling over crags, cliffs or into crevasses put the rope on in plenty of time.

10. Moving parallel to steep ground. If you are, for example, traversing round the head wall of a corrie or cwm, rope up as shown in Fig. (45).

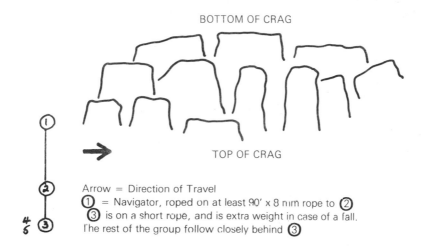

BOTTOM OF CRAG

TOP OF CRAG

Arrow = Direction of Travel
① = Navigator, roped on at least 90' x 8 nim rope to ②
③ is on a short rope, and is extra weight in case of a fall.
The rest of the group follow closely behind ③

Fig. (45). Roping-up when parallel to steep ground.

As already mentioned, the conventional sign for crags must be treated with caution, as there are cases on Ordnance Survey maps where it has been placed the wrong way round.

11. Bear in mind that on a traverse there is a tendency to lose height; or, if you are aware of this, a tendency to overcorrect the other way.

12. Keep a steady pace, because:
—you keep continuity of speed which will help your estimate of time.
—in a group of 6 or more, frequent halts result in people getting scattered and in a lack of trust in the navigator.

13. Concentration. Serious navigation requires concentration. Don't allow people to stray in front or to the side, as they will pull you off course.

14. High wind. Keep off exposed ridges, and try to use the natural shape of the landscape for protection. It may be necessary to rope-up. It is safe enough to exert yourself against a strong wind if at any time you can turn round and retreat to safety with the wind behind you. The converse is not true. Also, a strong wind blowing across your direction of travel may easily blow you off course.

15. Deep snow. The easiest going will be on ridges and windward slopes. The worst will be in hollows and lee slopes.

16. Avalanches. A safe route will depend on recognising avalanche conditions, but this complex subject is outside the scope of this small book. As far as Britain is concerned, our most usual avalanche is the windslab which forms on lee slopes. Identifying windslab can be very difficult, as local features cause wind eddies and these eddies put windslab on the most unexpected places—even on slopes which are generally windward slopes. By keeping to ridges and windward slopes, the danger will be greatly reduced.

17. Sudden mist or cloud. If the mist or cloud suddenly comes in:
—take a compass bearing on the next point before you are enveloped in the cloud.
—if you are in any doubt as to where you are, try to get a fix before being enveloped.
—get the party together.
—small features in mist may look much bigger than they really are. For example, a small knoll 10 metres high (which may not be marked on the map) can loom up in the mist and look like something 50-60 metres high. This can be misleading.

18. White-out. This is a snow condition of appalling visibility where it is impossible to distinguish between the horizon and the ground; where it is not possible to tell what is, say, ten feet in front of you. There could be a vertical drop, flat ground or a hill—and you simply cannot see it. This may occur in conditions of high wind and driving snow, i.e. blizzard; it may equally well occur in very still conditions. Anyone going out regularly in snow conditions will come across this condition; and the following points will help.

(i) in order to get some feedback as to what is in front or to the sides, throw snowballs—seven to ten yards will be enough. This obviously does not work in a blizzard, but is of considerable practical help in still conditions.

(ii) ask people to walk on either side of you. This will give useful feedback, particularly if you are in a group large enough to spare two or three people on either side. If you have more out than that, it becomes unwieldly. A situation where this works well is where you are following a ridge. In white-out it is easy to wander off the crest, particularly if it is more of a broad spur than a sharp ridge. But with people out on the sides you will soon see what is happening: if you are on the crest, they will be below you.

(iii) white-out is broken up by features such as rocks and human beings. Look carefully for cairns which may mark paths, path junctions or tops of hills.

(iv) look very carefully at the map and use features which may normally be ignored. For example, a steepish descent/ascent of 30 metres on an otherwise shallow slope is a feature which is definitely useable, although on a nice sunny day it would not even be noticed. Having identified it on the map, use the compass plus estimates of time and paces to reach that feature: and then move on to the next one.

(v) consider what you have been doing and plot that on the map. You may know, for example, just two things: firstly, that for the last ten or fifteen minutes you have been walking on flat ground, and, secondly, the bearing. Put that bearing (converted to grid) on the map and move it around the area you think you are in. Where one long edge of the compass crosses flat ground will, probably, be the flat ground you have just crossed.

(vi) drawing an analogy from yacht navigation, a position may be an E.P. (Estimated Position) or a Fix. The latter is where there is no doubt at all that your position is correct (e.g. a good resection) and the E.P. is where there is doubt (e.g. two narrow angled backbearings giving an unsatisfactory resection). From a Fix you can head off in confidence; from an

E.P. you head off with less confidence, looking for the first opportunity to get a Fix or another E.P., and constantly aware that you may not have been where the E.P. put you. However the E.P. is a vital step, and must not be ignored just because it seems a bit woolly. They build up a picture as to where you are, and they enable you to work your way along until you get a Fix. Returning to mountain navigation, the same approach can be adopted; and the positions which are obtained in (iv) and (v) above can be treated in the same way as an E.P. is treated in yacht navigation.

19. Searching for a point. Where a group is approaching a point in bad visibility, the standard sweep search is normal procedure. All you do is, instead of walking bunched up, spread out in line abreast so as to maximise the chance of finding the point. Fig. (46) shows a group of 5 people walking on a bearing AB, sweep searching for point P.

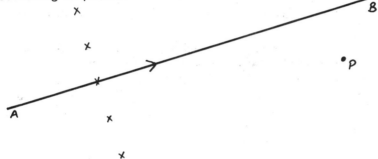

Fig. (46). Sweep search.

But someone on their own cannot, by definition, do a sweep search; and in that case the following method should be used:

—referring to Fig. (47), presume that you have been walking on a bearing AB, and that you are looking for point P. You could be anywhere on the line AB, but the time comes when you decide to stop and to search—point 'X' in Fig. (47).
—walk north for 10 paces.
—walk east for 10 paces.
—walk south for 20 paces.
—walk west for 20 paces.
—walk north for 30 paces.
—continue this pattern until the point is found.

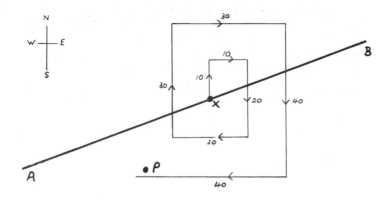

Fig. (47). Search by solo walker.

With this search pattern you will inevitably find the point. Depending on conditions, a factor of 15 or more paces may be suitable.

Answers to the exercise on Estimating Time and Paces

No.	Actual Time (mins.)	Actual Paces	No.	Actual Time (mins.)	Actual Paces
1.	29	1900	11.	20	1600
2.	20	1600	12.	40	2200
3.	30	2300	13.	30	2200
4.	36	2130	14.	14	1074
5.	18	2240	15.	35	—
6.	16	1000	16.	20	—
7.	26	1830	17.	30	—
8.	16	1450	18.	17	—
9.	20	1425	19.	10	—
10.	37	2870			

ALPINE GLACIER NAVIGATION

To navigate safely on glaciers and big Alpine snow fields obviously requires knowledge of snow, glaciers and avalanches.

This in itself is a huge subject and outside the scope of this small book.

DIFFERENCES BETWEEN BRITISH AND CONTINENTAL MAPS

1. If you open a Swiss map (Carte Nationale de la Suisse) or an Austrian map (Alpenvereinskarte), you will probably be impressed by the three dimensional effect. The map is almost a photograph. The ridges and glaciers are very obvious.

Much of this is due to shading. For example, the Swiss maps have the slopes facing north and west shaded lighter than those facing south and east.

2. Grid Lines. Austrian maps do not have them, which means that taking compass bearings is slightly more haphazard. And you cannot give a grid reference. Swiss maps have grid lines, but they use a different numbering system.

3. Magnetic Variation. This is much less than in Britain and for practical purposes is ignored. It is not worth bothering about a variation of, say, two degrees, when you could make that error in (a) taking the bearing, and (b) following the bearing.

4. Ski Routes. On the Swiss 1:50,000 and the Austrian 1:25,000 for the main areas, you have a choice between a map with or without ski routes. The ski routes are marked in red, and are recommended routes for winter and spring tourers. On the back of the map is a short description in guide book form, giving approximate times.

ACCURACY OF GLACIER INFORMATION

A glacier is a moving river of ice, continually being fed from the top and sides while melting at the bottom. All the time it is moving, so that if you fall into a crevasse at the top of a glacier, you will eventually come out at the bottom (the snout).

If the balance between feeding and melting is equal, the glacier keeps its shape. If the balance is unequal, the glacier will be either advancing or retreating. In the Alps, some are advancing, some are retreating and some are stable. If the glacier you are on is not stable, and if the survey was last done several years ago (as is often the case), you may have some problems. For example:

1. The snout (end of the glacier) may be a long way further back than indicated on the map—easily as much as 200 vertical metres or one kilometre horizontally. An example of this is the Sulztal glacier in the Stubai Alps of Austria.

2. A guide book may advise a summer route which goes up the glacier for a while and then takes to the rocks on the side. If the glacier has retreated, the rocks which have subsequently been exposed may be unclimable; and your route to the next hut starts to take on different dimensions.

3. A hut which was once built by the side of the glacier may now be left perched well above it. For example, the Concordia Hut in the Bernese Oberland of Switzerland has a very exciting section of vertical ladders leading up to it.

4. Crevasses which are marked on the map may not be there. More important, a glacier which is marked as being crevasse free may become heavily crevassed, for example the top section of the Otemma glacier just below the Pigne d'Arolla in Switzerland. A year or two later, they may have gone.

PLANNING A ROUTE

1. To avoid some of the problems just mentioned, take local advice—e.g. hut guardians and mountain guides. It helps greatly if you speak their language even if they speak English.

2. Having taken this advice, it is usually necessary to interpret it for your own needs. I have often asked advice, but have seldom been asked in return what seems to me to be an obvious question: "What is the experience of your party?" Invariably the advice errs on the safe side, but in one notable exception I found myself making an exciting ski descent in avalanche conditions of the Titzentalerweg, which is the summer route between Vent and the Hochjoch Hospiz in the Otztal Alps of Austria.

3. Plan to avoid the sides of glaciers where possible. There are more crevasses there, and there is also the danger of stonefalls and avalanches.

4. Plan to move from one identifiable point to another—e.g. rocks, ridges, huts, ends of glaciers etc.

PRACTICAL POINTS

1. Having planned to keep to the middle of the glacier to avoid the crevasses, stonefalls and avalanches, you may find in bad visibility that you have to go to the side to pick up an identifiable point—e.g. a rock ridge coming down to the glacier.

2. Try to keep as straight a line as possible, particularly on skis, and any turns should be open ones—for the benefit of people following you.

3. If you have to cross snow and ice avalanches, cross quickly and avoid making a turn near them.

Inevitably, avalanche debris has to be crossed. Identify the debris as to snow or ice, and then look to see where it has come from. It may be snow, or it may be ice from a fallen serac. The snow debris may well have frozen into very awkward lumps, and the ice will certainly be difficult to cross. If there is a danger of a further avalanche and if it looks as though the crossing of the debris will take a long time, an alternative route might be advised. Often snow debris indicates safety, on the argument that the avalanche has brought down the unstable snow and that the remaining snow is stable. On the other hand, if a fallen serac has scattered lumps of ice across your path, it is likely that any remaining seracs will do the same, particularly when the air temperature is high, as at midday and early afternoon.

4. Equally inevitably, potential avalanches sometimes have to be crossed. The same advice applies: cross fast, one at a time, and try to avoid turning on skis near them. Those on safe ground should watch those crossing in case they are avalanched.

5. An altimeter is invaluable when skiing down glaciers. On skis you lose height very quickly; and if you are not careful you find you have gone too far in the wrong direction and have to climb back up.

In the example (Fig. 48) in order to ski down from A to B, you would take the dotted line.

At first this keeps to the left, to avoid the crevasses on the right. At 3,000 m. it moves to the right to avoid more crevasses. (Altimeter useful).

If you failed to move to the right, you would end up at X. After maybe extracting yourself from a crevasse, you would have to climb nearly all the way back to 3,000 m. in order to get round the crevasses.

What took 20 mins. to descend could take 2 hours to re-ascend. Add the time to get out of the crevasse and you could spend a night there.

An altimeter is invaluable for making the turn at 3,000 m.

Fig. (48). Use of an altimeter on a glacier.

5. If in bad visibility you come to a crevasse in front of you:

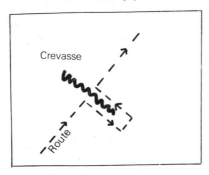

—move off at right angles to the compass course.
—measure this distance by rope lengths.
—after crossing the crevasse, move back the same distance on the other side, and resume the compass course.

Fig. (49). Negotiating a crevasse in bad visibility.

6. When planning to later descend the glacier you are going up:
—note carefully the position of crevasses while ascending the glacier.
—small marker flags can be useful if the weather looks like deteriorating. Mark crevasses, necessary turns and anything else which might be useful in a descent in bad weather.
—while descending, keep close to the uphill track if it hasn't been blown in or unless snow conditions dictate otherwise. For example, north facing slopes will hold powder longer in the day than south facing ones, and the skier will look for the powder. A small depression or ridge off to one side of the uphill track may offer better conditions later in the day.

7. Crevasses. Expect to find them where the ice is under tension —e.g. on the inside of bends, where rock ridges extend into the glacier, and where the glacier falls more steeply.

THE AUTHOR

Peter Cliff was born in Crayke, York, in 1943. He was educated at Rugby School, and then spent a year travelling abroad with various jobs in Africa, Australia and New Zealand. In 1963 he went to Southampton University and took a LL.B., after which he went into industry.

In 1970 he joined Outward Bound as an instructor working mainly at Moray but also at the three German Outward Bound schools. He then took a Certificate of Education at Bangor University, after which he worked for four years in Edinburgh as an outdoor instructor.

He has climbed in many areas of Britain and the Alps, Arctic Lapland and the Himalayas. His particular interest is ski-mountaineering, being a member of the 1972 British Alpine Ski Traverse and the 1976 Kulu (Himalaya) Ski Mountaineering Expedition.

He is married, and runs his own outdoor activity centre at Grantown-on-Spey in the Scottish Highlands. Details of the courses, which include hillwalking and mountaineering, are obtainable from Peter Cliff, Ardenbeg, Grant Road, Grantown-on-Spey, Morayshire PH26 3LD.